Nineteenth Annual Report of the Columbia Institution for the Deaf and Dumb for the Year Ending June 30, 1876

Gallaudet University Archives

Nineteenth Annual Report of the Columbia Institution for the Deaf and Dumb for the Year Ending June 30, 1876

ISBN/EAN: 9783337817268

Printed in Europe, USA, Canada, Australia, Japan

Cover: Foto ©Thomas Meinert / pixelio.de

More available books at **www.hansebooks.com**

NINETEENTH ANNUAL REPORT

OF THE

COLUMBIA INSTITUTION

FOR THE

DEAF AND DUMB

FOR THE

YEAR ENDING JUNE 30, 1876.

WASHINGTON:
GOVERNMENT PRINTING OFFICE.
1876.

NINETEENTH ANNUAL REPORT

OF THE

COLUMBIA INSTITUTION

FOR THE

DEAF AND DUMB

FOR THE

YEAR ENDING JUNE 30, 1876.

WASHINGTON:
GOVERNMENT PRINTING OFFICE.
1876.

COLUMBIA INSTITUTION FOR THE DEAF AND DUMB.

OFFICERS OF THE INSTITUTION.

Patron.—ULYSSES S. GRANT, President of the United States.
President.—EDWARD M. GALLAUDET, Ph. D., LL. D.
Secretary.—WILLIAM STICKNEY, Esq.
Treasurer.—GEORGE W. RIGGS, Esq.

Directors.—HON. GEORGE F. EDMUNDS, Senator from Vt.; HON. HENRY L. DAWES, of Mass.; HON. JOHN T. HARRIS, M. C. from Virginia; HON. WILLIAM A. WHEELER, M. C. from New York; HON. WILLIAM E. NIBLACK, of Ind.; REV. BYRON SUNDERLAND, D. D.; JAMES C. McGUIRE, Esq., HON. HENRY D. COOKE.

COLLEGE FACULTY.

President and Professor of Moral and Political Science.—EDWARD M. GALLAUDET, Ph. D., LL. D.
Professor of Mental Science and English Philology.—SAMUEL PORTER, M. A.
Professor of History and Ancient Languages.—EDWARD A. FAY, M. A.
*Professor of Modern Languages**— ——— ———.

Professor of Natural Science.—REV. JOHN W. CHICKERING, JR., M. A.
Professor of Mathematics and Chemistry.—JOSEPH C. GORDON, M. A.
Tutors.—J. BURTON HOTCHKISS, M. A.; AMOS G. DRAPER, M. A.
Lecturer on Natural History.—REV. WILLIAM W. TURNER, Ph. D.
Instructor in Art.—PETER BAUMGRAS.

FACULTY OF THE PRIMARY DEPARTMENT.

President.—EDWARD M. GALLAUDET, Ph. D., LL. D.
Instructors.—JAMES DENISON, M. A., Principal; MELVILLE BALLARD, M. S.; MARY T. G. GORDON.

Instructor in Articulation.—REV. JOHN W. CHICKERING, JR., M. A.
Instructor in Art.—PETER BAUMGRAS.

DOMESTIC DEPARTMENT.

Attending Physician.—N. S. LINCOLN, M. D.
Matron.—MISS ANNA A. PRATT.

Assistant Matron.—MISS MARGARET ALLEN.
Master of Shop.—ALMON BRYANT.

---

* The duties of this professorship are for the present discharged by the professor of history and ancient languages.

NINETEENTH ANNUAL REPORT

OF THE

COLUMBIA INSTITUTION FOR THE DEAF AND DUMB.

COLUMBIA INSTITUTION FOR THE DEAF AND DUMB,
KENDALL GREEN, NEAR WASHINGTON, D. C.,
October 25, 1876.

SIR: In compliance with the acts of Congress making provision for the support of this institution, we have the honor to report its progress during the year ending June 30, 1876.

NUMBER OF PUPILS.

The pupils remaining in the institution on the 1st day of July, 1876, numbered	64
Admitted during the year	12
Since admitted	24
Total	100

Under instruction since July 1, 1875, males 85; females 15. Of these 53 have been in the collegiate department, representing twenty States and the Federal District, and 47 in the primary department. A list of the names of the pupils connected with the institution since July 1, 1875, will be found appended to this report.

HEALTH OF THE INSTITUTION.

We are permitted to record another year of exemption from any prevailing disease. The only serious illness among our pupils was an isolated case of cerebro-spinal meningitis, which terminated fatally, in February last.

DEATH OF JAMES A. RUTHERFORD.

In the death of Mr. James A. Rutherford, whose illness has just been alluded to, our college sustained a serious loss. The following minute from the records of the faculty will show in how high esteem Mr. Rutherford was held by those who knew him best:

In the death of James A. Rutherford, the college has lost a member whose course commended him to the favorable notice of the faculty, and whose example, both as a young man and as a student, was valuable to his associates.

Though he had been for years assailed by serious disease, his progress in learning was praiseworthy. He possessed a logical mind, tenacious of its own conclusions, yet coupled with so clear a judgment as to render him eminently teachable.

He had a gentle disposition; he endeared himself to all by his unfailing good temper; and his name was without reproach.

While, therefore, the faculty sorrowfully acquiesce in the wisdom of that Providence who has seen fit to close his mortal career, they would bear testimony to his worth, and record their opinion that had his life and health been spared, he would have risen steadily to a position of honor and usefulness among his fellow-men.

COURSE OF STUDY.

The courses of study pursued in the several departments have remained essentially the same as in previous years. The following schedule and statements will show the branches taught:

IN THE PRIMARY DEPARTMENT.

During the first and second years of instruction: Elementary Lessons for the Deaf and Dumb, by Harvey Prindle Peet, LL. D.; First Lessons for the Deaf and Dumb, by John R. Keep, M. A.; The School Reader, part first, by Chas. W. Sanders, M. A.

During the third and fourth years: Lessons for Children, by Mrs. Barbauld; Reading without Tears, part second, by Miss Mortimer; Felter's Primary Arithmetic; Primary Geography, by Fordyce A. Allen, M. A.

During the fifth and sixth years: Primary History of the United States, by G. P. Quackenboss, A. M.; Common School History of the World, by S. G. Goodrich; First Lessons in English Grammar, by Simon Kerl, M. A.; New Intermediate Geography, by S. Augustus Mitchell; Felter's Intermediate Arithmetic.

Instruction is given through the whole course in the structure of the English sentence, and in penmanship according to the Spencerian system.

IN THE COLLEGIATE DEPARTMENT.

Preparatory course of study.

LOWER PREPARATORY YEAR.

Language.—The elements of English Grammar are studied throughout the year. The properties and forms of the parts of speech are taught, and in their combination in simple forms of construction. Parsing is begun. Symbols and diagrams are employed.

Mathematics.—Arithmetic is studied throughout the year. Special attention is given to fractions, percentage, including interest in all its forms, proportion, involution, and evolution. Students are required to analyze thoroughly every subject, the aim being to enable them to solve examples by reasoning upon the principles involved without recourse to set rules.

Natural Science.—Physical Geography is studied one term, and Natural philosophy two terms.

History.—Berard's History of England, as far as to the end of the reign of Henry VII, is used as an auxiliary to the study of grammar; and, in addition, the study of the history of the United States for one term is contemplated.

ADVANCED PREPARATORY YEAR.

Language.—English Grammar, as studied in the lower preparatory year, is reviewed, and a more minute examination of the parts of speech in their relations to each other is pursued, as a half or alternating study, for two terms. Analysis is studied in the third term. Parsing, in varying forms, is constantly exacted, and the student is required to explain examples given in the text-book, to construct some himself, and to select others from the companion study, Berard's History of England, and from other sources. Diagrams and symbols are used to present parsing and analysis in a concise form.

Latin is studied throughout the year. The first term is devoted to its etymology, the second to its distinctive grammatical features, and the third to its syntax. In the last term, about half of the first book of Cæsar's Gallic War is gone over.

Mathematics.—Loomis's Treatise on Algebra is the text-book, which is studied throughout the year. Quadratic equations are completed in the third term, and Algebra is then discontinued until the last term of the Freshman year. The method of instruction is similar to that employed in arithmetic. Much attention is given to the elucidation of problems, many of which are taken from Todhunter's Algebra and other sources. In comprehending these, some deaf-mutes labor under peculiar difficulties, not from lack of reasoning power, but from defective training in English during their primary instruction.

History.—Berard's History of England is a half-study, alternating with English Grammar. Illustrations of the principles enunciated in the Grammar are sought out, words are defined, idiomatic phrases are explained, and peculiar constructions are elucidated, by parsing, and by diagrams and symbols. A thorough mastery of the text is expected, and a knowledge of the geographical features of countries mentioned, and their location, is required. Outline-maps are drawn, and strict attention to the chronology is enforced. This class reads from the beginning of the reign of Henry VIII to the end of the 18th century.

UNDERGRADUATE COURSE OF STUDY.

I.—*Language.*

MODERN LANGUAGES.

English.—The Freshmen devote a portion of the first term to the analysis of English sentences, applying the principles to examples taken from their general reading and from Berard's History of England, which is studied in conjunction with grammar. The attention is given principally to the more difficult and complicated constructions of the English language. It is hoped that it will not be long before this study will be completed in the Preparatory Course.

History of the English language.—Text-book: Trench's English, Past and Present; third term of the Sophomore year. The students bring in on paper an epitome of the topics in the lesson, and give, further, a detailed statement, paragraph by paragraph, followed by answers to questions, and supplemented by explanations on the part of the teacher. For the review, a set of questions is given out, to be answered in writing at the recitations. Some use is made of the Brief History of the English Language, by Hadley, prefixed to Webster's Dictionary.

History of English literature.—The text-books are the Smaller History of English and American Literature, which is based upon Shaw's Manual, and the choice specimens, &c., prepared as an accompaniment. The study is begun the first term of the Sophomore year, and resumed the second term of the Senior year. With recitations from the historical compend, selections from the specimens are made the subject of critical study. An entire work of some author is occasionally selected for perusal and critical analysis, the result to be given in writing. Now and then an essay is required, giving an estimate of some author, as derived from sources outside of the text-book.

English composition.—Frequent exercises in original composition are required of students in all the classes, which are revised and returned with corrections and remarks.

French and German.—Both French and German are required in the course, French being studied in the Junior, and German in the Senior year, with daily recitations during the first and second terms, and alternate recitations during the third term. It is not so much attempted to teach these languages conversationally as to give a thorough comprehension of their grammatical forms and principles, the peculiarities of their idioms, and their relations to English, and especially to render the students skillful, accurate, and ready in translation. In French, Otto's Grammar and Bôcher's Reader are used during the first and second terms; in the third term, Racine's *Athalie*, Souvestre's *Philosophe sous les Toits*, or one of Erckmann-Chatrian's *Romans Nationaux*, is read. The corresponding course in German consists of Whitney's Grammar and Reader, followed by Fouqué's *Undine*, Lessing's *Minna von Barnhelm*, or Schiller's *Wilhelm Tell*.

ANCIENT LANGUAGES.

Latin.—There are daily recitations in Latin throughout the Freshman year and the first term of the Sophomore year. During the second and third terms of the Sophomore year, Latin is a half study, alternating with recitations in history. In the Freshman year, Sallust's Catiline or Jugurtha, and several of Cicero's orations, are read; in the Sophomore year, a part of Virgil's Æneid and the Odes of Horace. Special attention is paid to the construction and analysis of the language, and to its etymology in its bearings upon our own tongue. At the same time precision and elegance in translation are aimed at, and the endeavor is made to interest the students as much as possible in the subjects to which the text relates. While the authors read are for the most part such as the Faculty would prefer, if the circumstances of the case permitted, to confine to the Preparatory Course, and while—owing to the prominence given to French and German and the critical study of English—the proportion of time devoted to the ancient languages is less than in the usual curriculum of American colleges, it is believed that Latin is taught in such a manner as to awaken in the students the true spirit of classical scholarship, and enable them subsequently to read more difficult authors independently, with pleasure and profit.

Greek.—The study of Greek is optional; the course marked out by the Faculty, comprising Boise's First Lessons, Hadley's Grammar, and Xenophon's Anabasis, in the Freshman year, Homer's Iliad in the Sophomore year, and Demosthenes on the Crown in the Junior year, has been successfully pursued to a greater or less extent by several students.

II.—*Mathematics.*

Geometry.—The Freshman Class, in its first two terms, is taken through the first eight books of Loomis's Geometry. Demonstrations are occasionally made in writing, but the usual course is for the student to draw a diagram, and to give the proof by means of signs and the manual alphabet, pointing out each angle, line, &c., as it is needed in the argument. Several weeks are devoted to the demonstration of theorems not demonstrated in the text-book. In the examination upon the first six books, only the numbers of the book and of the proposition are given to the student; in the remaining books, the theorems are given.

Geometry is completed in the third term of the Freshman year. The spherical black-board is used in the discussion of spherical triangles.

Algebra is resumed, and the subjects of ratio and proportion, progressions, permutations, the binomial theorem, series, and the general theory of equations are studied. The recitations are chiefly written, and the students elucidate their work by means of the sign-language and manual English.

Conic Sections are studied in the first term of the Sophomore year. Sixty-five propositions are demonstrated, numerical exercises are solved, and a few theorems are assigned for original work.

Plane Trigonometry and Logarithms are studied in the second term. The text-book is well supplied with exercises, which are used to test the knowledge and comprehension of the class.

Spherical Trigonometry is studied in the third term. The method is the same as in plane trigonometry. In some classes the work has been abridged, and the time devoted to Mensuration and Surveying.

Mechanics.—All the elementary propositions of mechanics are mathematically demonstrated, and illustrated by numerous practical examples. The Juniors study mechanics for one term.

The principles of mechanics as applied to astronomy are studied by the Juniors in the third term, as noted under the head of Natural Science.

III.—*Natural Science.*

Chemistry.—The Sophomores memorize an elementary text-book to gain a knowledge of the principles, theories, symbols, and nomenclature of the subject. This work is accompanied or followed by illustrative experiments, which include the course recommended by Dr. Frankland.

Practical Chemistry.—The Juniors are required to do laboratory work, following the syllabus prescribed for the elementary stage in the English scientific examination at South Kensington. Elliot and Storer's work is the text-book in qualitative analysis, which is begun in the last term of the Junior year. The Juniors take notes of the work performed, and submit monthly reports. The laboratory is fitted up with necessary apparatus and instruments of research, and contains the principal chemicals and books of reference needed in chemical study.

Natural Philosophy.—The Juniors study hydrostatics, pneumatics, magnetism, electricity, heat and light, for one term, as set forth in Snell's Olmstead's College Philosophy. The apparatus in the laboratory affords the means of illustrating the principal phenomena, and students are expected to make the experiments themselves, as far as possible.

Astronomy, begun in the third term of the Junior year, is completed in the first term of the Senior year. The students are expected to master Loomis's Treatise, and are encouraged to consult other works of a descriptive and popular character.

Botany occupies two terms of the Sophomore year, and students are required to sustain an examination in physiological and structural botany, and also to be able to describe fully and determine the names of ordinary plants, excluding only a few of the more difficult families.

Zoology.—One term of the Junior year is devoted to the elements of zoology, including the general principles of classification.

Mineralogy.—Junior year, one term: Dana's Mineralogy, Foye's Tables. Mineralogy has been omitted by a few classes for want of time, but an effort will be made to give to the subject the attention it should have as an introduction to geology. The course embraces a general view of the subject, with practice in the identification of the more common minerals.

Geology is taken up during the first term of the Senior year, and *Physiology* during the second term.

The course then closes with the Relations of Man to his Environment. as set forth in Guyot's Earth and Man.

Whenever practicable, use is made in this department of one of Beck's binocular microscopes, with the manipulation of which the students are familiarized.

Morton's college-lantern is also employed for purposes of illustration.

IV.—*History.*

English History.—The history of the nineteenth century is taken up during the first term of the Freshman year, and, as in the Preparatory Classes, is made subservient to the study of grammar.

Ancient History.—The study of Thalheimer's Manual occupies the second and third terms of the Freshman year, and includes a brief survey of the minor monarchies of the ancient world and a detailed study of the four great empires—Egypt, Persia, Greece, and Rome. The geography and chronology are pursued with thoroughness, the drawing of maps and the construction of chronological charts being required, while occasional essays upon some character or event that will demand contemporaneous reading are exacted. The student is also encouraged to apply the knowledge obtained in this study to his reading of the classical authors.

Mediæval and *Modern History* are taught in alternation with Latin during the second and third terms of the Sophomore year, the text-book from which recitations are made being Thalheimer's Manual. While the text-book is thoroughly committed to memory, additional information upon the subjects treated is imparted by the Professor in connection with the recitations, and the students are encouraged to undertake as much collateral reading as their time will permit.

The *Philosophy of History* is taught in the third term of the Junior year, alternating with French. Guizot's History of Civilization is made the text-book, and the students are required to present the results of their outside reading upon historical subjects in carefully-prepared essays.

V.—*Philosophy and Political Science.*

Logic.—Second term, Junior year: Twenty-one chapters of Jevons's Lessons in Logic are thoroughly studied, with practice upon a large part of the examples at the end of the volume, besides requiring original ones to be given.

Rhetoric.—First term, Junior year: The text-book is Hart's Composition and Rhetoric, with some use of other authors. Pains are taken to fix and familiarize the principles by careful study of examples, with construction of some original ones on the part of the student. A set of questions is given out for the review.

Mental Science.—During the third Senior term, the more important portions of Porter's Intellectual Science are studied, with aid from the professor as required by subjects of so abstract a nature.

Moral Philosophy.—During seven weeks of the first term the Seniors have a daily exercise in this study, reading the whole of Haven's Moral Philosophy. Questions are asked on each day's portion of the text-book, and comments are made by the Professor.

Evidences of Christianity.—During four weeks of the first term and three weeks of the second term the Seniors have a daily recitation in Butler's Analogy. Dr. Emory's Analysis is used, and made the basis of questions. The book is studied without omissions.

Political Economy.—Perry's text-book is used, with a daily exercise, for nine weeks of the second term of the Senior year.

International Law.—Woolsey's text-book is read, with a daily recitation, during about eight weeks of the third term, Senior year. The introduction to Calvo's *Le Droit International*, translated by the Professor, is also read by the class and made the subject of examination.

Æsthetics.—Bascom's Lectures on the Science of Beauty are read during the last month of the Senior year, with a daily recitation accompanied by brief lectures from the Professor.

Miscellaneous.

Instruction in Book-keeping and in Drawing and Painting is given to those who desire it.

Instruction in Articulation is given to those semi-mutes who desire it, and to such congenital deaf-mutes as are judged to give sufficient promise of success in this department. For these latter, the "Visible-Speech" method of Professor Bell has been found to be a great help. In some cases, practice in articulation is afforded by oral recitations in the regular course.

EXERCISES OF PRESENTATION-DAY.

The exercises of the regular public anniversary of our collegiate department took place April 26 in the Hall of the institution, and were attended by a very large number of visitors.

After prayer by the Rev. S. S. Mitchell, D. D., of Washington, the candidates for degrees delivered original essays, as follows:

Oration, "Our Educational Progress," by George M. Teegarden, Centreville, Iowa.

Dissertation, "The Study of History," by Dudley W. George, Danville, Kentucky.

Oration, "Pictures of Creation," by William G. Jones, New York City.

Oration, "The Influence of Mathematical Studies upon Personal Character," by Amos G. Draper, B. A., Aurora, Illinois.

ORATION BY AMOS G. DRAPER, B. A.

Mathematics is distinguished among the sciences by the certainty which attends its operations and conclusions. The ideas it presents are so distinct, its reasonings so self-evident, that it affords the most certain knowledge with which the mind is conversant. The meaning of its definitions, the truth of its axioms, and the correctness of the results at which it arrives, are matters concerning which there cannot be the slightest doubt or difference of opinion. While observation and experiment may deceive and confuse, demonstration ends in clear and absolute knowledge.

This exactness of the science has made it a chief instrument of human activity. A noble steamship, fresh from the builder's hands, resting lightly upon her native waters and ready to speed to other shores, is hailed as a triumph. She is but a combination of solidified mathematical theorems. We see a still greater triumph when she urges her way out upon the illimitable ocean, and pursues an undeviating course, day after day and week after week, finally to reach her destined port with unfailing precision. Mathematics again enabled her so to do.

The same instrumentality that empowered mankind to map out the highways of the sea has built those of the land—bridging chasms, tunneling mountains, and striding across rivers. It has fashioned the vehicles that course upon those highways, together with the innumerable machines by which labor is lessened, food and clothing are cheapened, buildings perfected, and conveniences of all kinds multiplied.

Nor is this all. After covering the earth with a net-work of improvements, and diving into its bowels to bring up the metals that enrich and the gems that adorn, it has rendered man competent to turn intelligent eyes upon the starry spaces above and establish the relations and movements of the orbs which circle around us. A brilliant though still but a single example of its powers may be seen in the achievement of Leverrier, whose mind, aided by its principles, passed beyond the borders of our then recognized system, and there pointed out accurately the position, path, and magnitude of a world before unknown.

Clearly the *utility* of mathematical studies can scarcely be overrated. Their value as a mental discipline, also, will not be gainsaid. Philosophers are agreed that they develop and strengthen some of the most important faculties of the mind. It is not disputed, even by those who have endeavored to belittle such studies, that, for instance, they sharpen and concentrate the attention, augment the power of consecutive thought, evoke, exercise, and invigorate the reason; for in these studies the constant presence and action of attention, consecutive thought, and the reasoning faculty, is obviously the price of even the smallest real success.

Therefore, not lingering upon these points, we may be impelled to go beyond and above them, and to inquire as to the effect of such studies upon personal character. Do they tend to elevate the moral as well as develop the mental faculties; to cherish love of order and reverence for law; to deepen the sense of responsibility and establish faith; in a word, to make men better in life and happier in death?

When we reflect upon the qualities that indicate excellence of character, two stand pre-eminent. The first is *decision*. "Character," says Novalis, "is a perfectly formed will." He who has it not only has opinions, habits of thought, and courses of action, but has them all decidedly; and the influence of his voice and example impresses them upon his fellows. The second quality is *benevolence*, which alone can restrain the man of firm will from unjust acts. A man of noble character ever seeks to help and never to harm; therefore, if a man fail in decision or lack benevolence, whatsoever else may be his claims to distinction, even though æsthetics refine his tastes to the utmost, and though all science exalt his mind, and though all honors cluster about his name, he deserves not the title and wins not the homage gladly accorded to a man of the highest character.

Now, a slight consideration of the nature of mathematical studies is sufficient to convince that they are peculiarly calculated to heighten decision of character. Since in them the mind advances to a final decision by a series of minor decisions, each of them unquestionable because based upon the irrefragable testimony of intuition—since, in fine, it is the very province of our science *to decide*, without the smallest danger of error, it would be strange indeed if a mind impressed and led by such a species of knowledge did not absorb and retain something of the consistency and firmness embodied in its principles.

When, however, we ascend still higher in the scale of our inquiry, and attempt to ascertain the influence of these studies upon moral qualities in their highest development as religious character, the view is less clear. Indeed, it has been argued by some philosophers, notably by Sir William Hamilton, that mathematical studies lead to skepticism, and disbelief in the first truths of natural religion.

But his arguments appear to be based upon a consideration of the effect of studies in *pure* mathematics alone. There is scarcely any study which, so viewed, would not be deemed comparatively worthless. What should we think of chemistry or of botany if we considered these sciences merely as labyrinths of rules and recorded experiments, instead of avenues revealing the wonders of the globe? Or of grammar, if it were merely the body of its formal laws, and not a means of acquaintance with the thoughts and lives of men in all ages? And if it be unreasonable so to consider them, how can we decide fairly as to the influence of mathematics without weighing it, also, in connection with what it reveals to us in its manifold applications?

Hamilton's argument proceeds on a second assumption not more warrantable, namely, that these studies are pursued to the neglect of others. We would claim for them no such preference. High character is a normal, rounded whole. Whoever has it, is "*in scipso totus teres atque rotundus;*" and to secure it the man must be developed on all sides.

The way being thus cleared, there is firm ground for a well-founded belief that mathematical studies, in what they unfold to our knowledge, point unmistakably to the existence of a Deity; and more, they identify humanity with that Deity, and strongly confirm the testimony of consciousness that, whatever may be the fortunes of human life, that life is incessantly laying up in other realms the records of its acts, its pernicious failures, and its beneficent successes.

In the human mind there is an innate appreciation of *symmetry*.

As children making their first rude attempts at drawing with only sticks on the sand, so men yet ignorant of science strive to develop regular forms and avoid irregularities and excrescences.

Children, with eyes and ears opened wide, are filled with admiration by regularity of outline, beauty of color, and harmony of sound. Long before the sciences that mark our present civilization were known, the first children of the earth, the first men, cultivated this kind of knowledge. The intellectual life of our race began, as that of each individual begins, in the appreciation of geometrical truths. The earliest Hindoos and Chinese of whom we have any records were familiar with the properties of the right-angled triangle, the discovery of which is commonly attributed to Pythagoras. And still, as civilization advances, and as children grow to manhood, the love of form, color, and harmony remains central among the passions which sway the soul with delight.

Whence do we derive this species of mental and æsthetic pleasure? Does it not flow from the instinctive but unrecognized perception of mathematical principles? The very essence of those principles is harmony, order, proportion. All of these are certainly essential to a tractive form. Though the connection is less obvious, enough is known to warrant the belief that the same principles underlie, also, and contribute to the charms of color and harmony.

But as knowledge of the universe increases, the more convincing becomes the evidence that an infinite intelligence is at work carrying forward certain of its plans in accordance with these exact principles. Men have delighted in symmetry from the beginning, without knowing that symmetry pervades created things. They constructed geometrical figures from natural models, but they did so before they knew that even the tiniest snowflake is also a geometrical figure. They observed that the leaves of a plant are distributed around the stem at regular intervals ages before it was discovered that the law which governs the distribution governs, also, the distances of the planets from the sun. Yet, even in ancient times, the evidence was so abundant and clear that Plato described the Creator as "a being who geometrizes continually."

And among modern philosophers, Herbert Spencer, though "famous for the strength with which he has maintained that we can assign to the First Cause of the universe no attributes whatever, asserts with equal strength and emphasis that the existence of the First Cause is forced constantly on our attention and avouched to us with a certainty that is attained by no other truth whatever."

It is evident that in mathematical investigations the human mind advances upon paths marked out by that mind which creates and sustains the universe. In this direction the conclusions of men, as far as they go, partake of the perfection of the intelligence whose works they ponder. They think after it the thoughts of that intelligence. In all the range of subjects that occupy the mental forces purely, it is to be doubted if there is one which so distinctly asserts the connection between the human and the creative mind, and displays them in reciprocal activity.

Yet the rank of the Great Teacher cannot be imperilled. The little that men can fathom of His thoughts but introduces them to sublimer subjects of contemplation. Those are humblest who have farthest advanced in endeavors to comprehend the mysteries of creation, and none realize so fully the force of the poet's question:

> "Why, what is this patient entrance into nature's deep resources
> But the child's most gradual learning to walk upright without bane?"

Mathematics, indeed, cannot define the moral character of that Deity whose existence it declares. But in consciousness the mind has an arbiter whose decisions are scarcely less authoritative than the intuitions of mathematics. Inspecting the lives of men in all generations, we cannot fail to see that they are prone to invest a deity with their own highest attributes. With the universal force that mathematical revelations convince mankind that there is intelligence akin to, yet beyond their own, with all that force, and with redoubled fervor, consciousness affirms that this intelligence embodies and inculcates the noblest sentiments felt by humanity.

And here mathematics can support the teachings of consciousness by most impressive warnings. One illustration must suffice on this occasion. Charles Babbage, in a chapter upon the permanence of words and actions, presents a view which, even if all his inferences be not accepted, can scarcely be contemplated without a thrill of admiration and fear.

Voices, indeed, quickly grow inaudible to human ears; the effects of actions seem to disappear; yet it is demonstrable that voices are taken up by every particle of the surrounding air and borne on to infinity; and it can be proved beyond cavil that physical actions are impressed upon the most distant spheres.

Thus each kindly-spoken word is transmitted in the volumes of the air; and each arm that falls in anger drags in its descent the stars from their courses.

However faint these tones may seem to be, however small these effects, it needs not different powers from our own, but only a finer sense, a keener mathematical analysis, to hearken to the one, weigh the other, and read, as in a clear-writ book, the records we make here.

After the conclusion of the essays presented by the candidates for degrees, the following addresses were delivered:

ADDRESS BY JOSEPH HENRY, LL. D., DIRECTOR OF THE SMITHSONIAN INSTITUTION, WASHINGTON.

I have accepted with much pleasure the invitation to attend the anniversary exercises of this College, since it gives me an opportunity to express my appreciation of the design of the establishment, the plan which has been adopted, and the manner in which it has thus far been executed.

Institutions for the education of the deaf and dumb illustrate in a striking manner the higher civilization of the present age in contrast with those of the past. In old times the deaf and dumb were considered in law as idiots, incapable of giving consent to any transaction, and were suffered to remain in the midst of communities of high intelligence, in regard to mental and moral culture, almost in a condition of barbarism. Deprived, except in a very limited degree, of the means of obtaining information other than that confined to the visible present within the range of their own observations, they were cut off from all knowledge of the past, from the sweet music of speech, and from all the finer emotions conveyed by the sympathy of sound. How great is the misfortune of one in civilized society who is unable to read, and how much more is he to be commiserated who, in addition to this, is unable to receive communications through verbal sounds! What a treasure to the human soul are books, those ships of knowledge, as Bacon has aptly called them, which, freighted with the intelligence of one age, are floated across the sea of time to another, uniting the past and the present, preserving the continuity of human history and human sympathy!

What an inestimable blessing was the teaching of these children of silence and of isolation to read, and furnishing them with the means of bringing their minds in unison with the thought, the feelings, and the emotions of their fellow-beings in all times and in all places.

It may be the boast of our centennial year that we have kept abreast of the world in this benevolent enterprise, and I may be allowed to remind the friends of this College, as a matter of congratulation, that the honored father of its president spent a laborious and successful life in advancing the cause which his son, with filial enthusiasm, is now extending to a higher development.

In 1864, a plan was submitted to me for examination, by the president of this Institution, of a graduated course, terminating in a collegiate curriculum. In my report upon the proposition I warmly recommended its adoption, as a means of increasing the enjoyment and extending the sphere of usefulness of the class intended to be benefited. I am now happy to say that the experiment has been successful. The scientific examination-papers of last year were submitted to me for report as to their character; while they involved the solution of questions in mathematics, physics, chemistry, geology, &c., requiring accurate knowledge and profound thought, *the answers were such as to do honor to the undergraduates of any college in this country.*

The deaf and dumb are not inferior to any other class in mental activity and power, and from the want of the sense of hearing are capable, perhaps, of more undisturbed attention and of sustained effort for the accomplishment of high mental achievement. They are specially well adapted to various scientific investigations, and may become successful laborers in the line of astronomy, heat, light, electricity, magnetism; in the great domain of chemistry and natural history; in short, in every branch of human thought, with the exception of that which relates to sound; and even in the theoretical part of this they may make advances beyond our present knowledge by deductions from the mathematical expressions which indicate the relation of sonorous waves to the forces which produce them. Why should they not, therefore, be educated to the full extent of their mental and physical capacity? The extension of their studies will certainly add to their pleasure, and prepare them as colaborers for extending the bounds of human thought. The plan proposed of giving a collegiate course in this institution has been, as I have said, eminently successful: it has been commended in foreign journals, and while the graduates have, in several instances, been employed in scientific calculations, one has received, on account of his attainments, an honorary degree from Dartmouth College.

For more fully carrying out the plan, however, additional means are required; a larger number of professors should be employed, and the implements of instruction should be increased. Visible illustrations of physical principles and phenomena should be amply supplied. The impressions made upon the mind through the eye are the most definite and lasting; and as this instrument of sense is the one principally employed by the deaf-mute, it is in a state of abnormal activity, and should therefore be furnished with all the appliances best calculated to render it most effective in the acquisition of knowledge.

The whole number of deaf-mutes in the country may be estimated at 25,000, and for the education of these a large number of teachers will be required. This College, with its extended curriculum, will be the most prominent establishment for furnishing laborers in this line.

Moreover, a considerable portion of the deaf and dumb are the offspring of wealthy parents, and the prospect of furnishing to these a higher course of mental culture will increase the number of pupils of this institution in proportion as its character is developed and the results of its instruction are made known. What parent would not purchase at any price the advantage to his child of an extended field of pleasure and of usefulness in a life of devotion to scientific investigations? What pleasure could a deaf-mute not receive from the practical use of the microscope, could a taste for investigations by means of that instrument be induced through his connection with this institution, and how greatly would that pleasure be enhanced were he able to add to the sum of human knowledge by original observations! There is pleasure in the acquisition of knowledge. There is also pleasure in being able to communicate to others the knowledge we have acquired; but the pleasure of *originating knowledge* is incomparably greater than either of these, and there is nothing in the physical constitution of the deaf and dumb which would preclude them from participation in this higher enjoyment. In order to this, however, the instruction should not be limited to scientific facts and principles, but should include scientific manipulation.

To foster and develop this Institution is an object worthy of the General Government. If properly sustained, it will do honor to our nation, and to those who conceived and assisted in developing its plan; and it will serve as an illustration of the benevolence of the age in which we live. That it may continue to prosper and bring forth fruit commensurate with the object of its foundation is my most earnest prayer.

ADDRESS BY DANIEL C. GILMAN, LL. D., PRESIDENT OF THE JOHNS HOPKINS UNIVERSITY, BALTIMORE, MD.

I can assure you, Mr. President, for my associates of the Johns Hopkins Foundation, who are here present, as well as for myself, that the pleasure we have enjoyed in witnessing the attainments of the young men who have been before us is not likely to be repeated or equaled until we have the pleasure of welcoming some one of them to the special and ampler advantages which are proffered by the new University in Baltimore.

As we came hither on the train this morning, we read the telegrams from Paris describing the brilliant assemblage which was held but yesterday in the capital of France to commemorate and perpetuate the ties of friendship between the Americans and the French. The immediate occasion of this demonstration, as you are all doubtless aware, was to secure the means to erect, in the harbor of New York, a colossal statue of Liberty, which should be a memorial to men from every clime of the alliance between France and the United States, by which our independence was achieved, and our civil liberty made secure. The historic names of Rochambeau, De Tocqueville, and Lafayette were represented on that occasion; and music and oratory inspired the audience with international enthusiasm.

In all this I rejoice. But it reminded me of another chapter of international good-will which should not be forgotten in this assemblage of those who are interested in the instruction of the deaf and dumb.

More than a hundred years ago a rare philanthropist of France, the Abbé de l'Epée, instituted those ingenious, beneficent, and fruitful methods for the education of the deaf-mute which, in their latest and fullest developments, are employed in this College.

Somewhat later a less renowned but not less honorable ecclesiastic of France, the Abbé Sicard, worthy successor of the Abbé de l'Epée, was engaged in carrying forward the agencies and devices for the enlightenment of those who have been deprived of the power of hearing and of speech. Sixty years ago a young New Englander, fresh from collegiate and professional studies, observed the intelligence of a deaf-mute child in Hartford, and soon discovered how quick she was to respond to the efforts which were made by signs to enlighten her intellectual and moral life. His success in teaching her attracted the notice of other philanthropists, and before long this young New Englander, whose name is now among the foremost of American teachers and well-doers, and is honorably borne by his son, the presiding officer of this College, was sent to Europe by his fellow-citizens in Hartford, to see and learn the methods there employed in communication with what had been the land of Silence. Repelled from England, he resorted to France, where, by the hand of the Abbé Sicard, he was initiated, with the quickness of a facile scholar, into the mysteries of the language of signs, and into the French discoveries respecting the education of deaf-mutes. Thus to France are we indebted for the beginning of a philanthropic movement which culminates in the College within whose walls we are assembled.

I am glad that the ties of French and American union are to be commemorated in New York. It is pleasant to look upon the figures of Washington and Lafayette, side by side, near the Speaker's chair in the national House of Representatives; but I hope that when some future writer shall describe the glories of New York or Washington, he will record the fact that not statesmen alone but philanthropists have been honored by picture and by bust. Then, doubtless, there will stand on Kendall Green a new memorial of French and American co-operation, carved in marble or modeled in bronze, to remind each student within these walls and each inquiring stranger of Sicard and Gallaudet, the Catholic and the Huguenot, the teacher and the scholar, by whose joint labors, once united and then far apart, this College has been made possible.

I congratulate you, ladies and gentlemen, on what we have this day observed in respect to the education of deaf-mutes, but I have had other and exceptional opportunities to know something of the progress of these students. Some days ago the examination papers in various branches of knowledge were submitted to me, and, without pretending to have read them thoroughly or to be competent to judge them all, I can repeat with emphasis the commendation from Professor Henry, to which you have just listened, and echo his remark, that *these papers would have been creditable to the students of any college in the land.*

Knowing something of the difficulties encountered by skillful teachers in training the minds of those who have the use of all their senses, I wonder at the success of those who teach only by appeals to the eye, while the portal of the ear, on which so many ordinary teachers exclusively rely, remains closed to their instructions.

I admire, moreover, the spirit which animates the education here imparted. These young men are not treated as unfortunates, to be the life-long objects of pity and charity, but as those who are providentially fettered by peculiar difficulties, or deprived of advantages which most persons possess. Their happiness may be the greater because of the very obstacles they overcome; their vision from the mountain-top may be clearer and more enjoyable than the prospect of those who plod along the valleys.

This is the first deaf-mute college in the world, but it is not the first time deaf-mutes have been admitted to college. I remember a passage in Stanley's Lectures on Canterbury, where he describes Queen's College at Oxford in the days of the famous Black Prince, and tells us that while the Master and twelve Fellows in the college-hall dined daily together, in commemoration of Christ and his apostles, the deaf and dumb and the blind were admitted to the door to receive their dole of cast-off morsels. How different this scene; how changed the times; how beneficent the progress! In the early days of our faith, when they saw the dumb to speak, "they glorified the God of Israel." Can we do less to-day?

So as we part, my friends, let us rejoice, as patriots, that here, first in all Christendom, a college for deaf-mutes has been begun where scholastic work is performed worthy of any college; let us rejoice, as teachers, at the demonstration that by the eye knowledge may be acquired as sound and as comprehensive as that which is ordinarily gained by eye and ear together; let us rejoice, as philanthropists, that those classes of our fellow-men who were once treated as miserable and inaccessible unfortunates, scarcely above the dumb animals, are now erect as men among their fellow-men; let us rejoice, as Christians, that the example of the Great Teacher has, in some degree, been imitated, who obliterated the barriers between the deaf man and his fellow-men and caused the dumb to speak.

ADDRESS BY HON. ZACHARIAH CHANDLER, SECRETARY OF THE INTERIOR, WASHINGTON.

I was not invited to make a speech. The contract was that I should say a word or two, and I shall not violate the contract.

It is true that this institution is nominally in charge of the Interior Department, and really it would be somewhat interfered with, in its running arrangements, if the Secretary of that Department should neglect to put his sign-manual on its requisitions for funds.

The cry has been raised, and it has become almost universal, of corruption! Corruption!! Corruption!!! To take up a portion of the newspaper-press of the country, and to listen to the cries uttered by a very large class, the belief would be that the devil had been chained one thousand years and had just been let loose. And the cry goes up for "the good old times," "the pure old times," "the upright, holy times," and other times. My friends, look at the advantages of these young men, and the efforts they have so successfully made before us. A hundred years ago the class to which they belong were neglected, and even ostracized. Do *they* want to go back to "the good old times?"—the good old times of darkness, despair, ignorance, and misery?

Shall we take away this and other benevolent institutions, where the blind, the sick, and the insane are cared for—the hospital and the asylum? Go into almost any State—I wish I could say every State, but certainly in most of the States—and you will find the fostering care of the State government spreading over all. We don't wish to go back to "the good old days."

I do not believe this world is growing worse, for I believe the world is better to-day than it was even one year ago. I believe it has gone ahead in every respect. The world is progressing daily toward purity, morality, honesty, and religion.

Now, let me say, whenever you find a man, or a set of men, or the newspaper-press, howling about "Corruption," "Corruption," "Corruption," look *inward* and you will find it there.

I congratulate you, Mr. President, and I thank our friends for being present to examine the progress made by the students of this College. Would to God that our legislators, one and all, could be present. I think they would not act niggardly in their appropriations for the support of this grand Institution.

The undergraduates who had delivered essays were then presented by the president of the institution to the board of directors as candidates for the degree of bachelor of arts. Mr. Amos G. Draper, B. A., was presented as a candidate for the degree of master of arts.

After which the exercises were closed with prayer and the benediction by Rev. I. L. Townsend, Chaplain of the House of Representatives.

CONFERRING OF DEGREES.

At the close of the academic year, degrees were conferred in accordance with the recommendations of presentation-day.

A VISIT FROM THE EMPEROR OF BRAZIL.

On Friday, June 2, an occasion of great interest occurred at Kendall Green, of which the following description appeared in the National Republican the ensuing day:

A little after 7 o'clock yesterday morning Dom Pedro d'Alcantara, Emperor of Brazil, accompanied by le Vicomte de Bom Retiro, chamberlain to His Majesty, and Señor A. P. de Carvalho Borges, Brazilian minister, visited the National College for Deaf Mutes, on Kendall Green, in the northeastern suburbs, where they were received by General John Eaton, the Commissioner of Education, by whom the officers of the institution were presented to the distinguished visitors.

President Gallaudet briefly explained the scope of the institution in answer to the Emperor's pertinent inquiries, while pupils from the primary department

WROTE ORIGINAL EXERCISES,

which the Emperor read and commended. Words of welcome were then written by representatives of the college classes. We can give only a few extracts. A freshman wrote: "We welcome you, not merely as a formality, nor because it is the first time a foreigner of so honorable and responsible a position as yourself has thus honored our institution, but because we desire that your visit shall be one of pleasure, interest, and profit. * * * Our only regret is that we have not the honor and pleasure of extending our welcome to Her Majesty the Empress. As you have come *early*, we kindly ask you to stay *late*." A sophomore wrote:

"WE ADMIRE YOUR POLICY,

activity, and the pleasure you are taking in your visit to our country. It would give us great pleasure to entertain you, and to make you a deaf-mute for a while, if thereby the mutes of Brazil might be benefited." Another student wrote: "The silent manifestations on every side speak louder than my words can of the cordial greeting extended to you, sire, and of the pleasure felt at your visit. Recognized as a strong and zealous advocate of learning, an eager participant in whatever tends toward the advancement of civilization—whose manifold blessings are already blooming in the sunny land of Brazil—we trust that this institution,

ONE OF CIVILIZATION'S FAIREST FRUITS,

will disclose to you the importance of its work—act as a plea for the deaf-mutes of your empire." A senior wrote: "It is a great privilege to be allowed to study, to learn, to be educated. Happiness requires it, beauty of character demands it, and pureness of spirit needs it." Another senior gave some entertaining examples of pantomime, after which the Emperor personally tested the attainments of some of the classes by exercises of an impromptu character in Latin, algebra, chemistry, and astronomy, and took, for future inspection, specimens of papers written by the students at the regular examinations.

Just before his departure the Emperor performed a beautiful act in a very graceful manner—

THE PLANTING OF AN IVY.

He received the vine from the hands of the venerable widow of the founder of the first deaf-mute institution in America—the voiceless mother of President Gallaudet—planted it skillfully, and plucked from it some leaves as a *souvenir* of his visit.

The Emperor seemed to be highly interested in all that he saw, and certainly his intelligence, appreciation, kindness, and sauvity won the hearts of all he met on Kendall Green.

EXCURSION OF STUDENTS AND PUPILS TO THE CENTENNIAL EXHIBITION.

It has been customary for several years to arrange for a picnic or pleasure excursion for the students and pupils on some Saturday in the early summer. This year an unusual gratification was afforded to those connected with the institution by the substitution of an excursion to the International Exhibition at Philadelphia for the usual picnic. Authority was given to the president to incur an expense not exceeding eight hundred dollars for the excursion, and on the closing day of the term, June 28, the students and pupils of both departments, under the charge of the president, assisted by several of the instructors, took a special car for Baltimore, via the Baltimore and Ohio Railroad. By the courtesy of the managers of this road, transportation was furnished at half the usual fare, and the car containing the party was drawn to the Light-street wharf in Baltimore, where one of the propellers of the Shriver Line was taken for Philadelphia. The managers of this line also afforded transportation at a very low rate, and the choice of the route gave the students and pupils an opportunity of a sail on the Chesapeake Bay, a passage through the Delaware Canal, and up the Delaware River.

The pupils of the primary department remained two days at Philadelphia, spending every available hour in the Exhibition. The students of the college were afforded three days in the Exhibition, some of them remaining longer at their own expense.

The degree of pleasure and amount of instruction afforded to those for whose benefit this excursion was undertaken can hardly be estimated, and expressions of delight and gratitude on their part were universal.

No misadventure occurred to interfere with the enjoyment of the occasion, excepting a few instances of slight indisposition, such as has been common in pilgrimages to the Centennial.

Expenditures.

The receipts and disbursements for the year now under review will appear from the following detailed statements:

I.—SUPPORT OF THE INSTITUTION.

Receipts.

Balance from old account	$3,991 81
Received from Treasury of the United States	48,000 00
Received from errors corrected	2 64
Received for board and tuition	3,322 64
Received from manual-labor fund	291 00
Received from students for books and stationery	364 94
Received for work done in shop	378 73
Received from sale of live stock	343 50
Received from damage to grounds by cattle	5 50
Received from sale of gas	47 25
Received from pupils for repairs to shoes	75
Received from sale of old lumber	10 00
Received from sale of old metal	46 00
Received from sale of old carpet	9 00
Total	56,813 76

Disbursements.

Expended for salaries and wages	$28,331 51
Expended for groceries	2,855 82
Expended for meats	4,020 35
Expended for household expenses, marketing, &c	1,637 64
Expended for butter and eggs	1,949 67
Expended for fuel	4,257 41

Expended for bread	$1,116 30
Expended for gas	1,065 75
Expended for repairs on buildings	1,512 54
Expended for furniture	908 67
Expended for live stock	315 00
Expended for expenses of directors' meetings	185 00
Expended for books and stationery	958 08
Expended for dry goods and shoes	305 98
Expended for medical attendance	142 00
Expended for plants and shrubs	122 15
Expended for feed, fertilizers, and seeds	495 87
Expended for lumber	1,162 85
Expended for printing and engraving	283 18
Expended for ice	103 71
Expended for drugs and chemicals	136 55
Expended for freight	22 28
Expended for carriage-hire	10 00
Expended for carriage and wagon repairs	44 63
Expended for exhibitions	67 00
Expended for illustrative apparatus	474 66
Expended for Centennial excursion	715 00
Expended for blacksmithing	65 02
Expended for harness and repairs	83 90
Expended for hardware	608 23
Expended for threshing-machine	220 00
Expended for carriage	500 00
Balance unexpended	2,137 01
Total	56,813 76

II.—EXTENSION AND FITTING UP OF BUILDINGS.

Receipts.

Balance from old account	$70 96
Received from Treasury of the United States	40,000 00
Total	40,070 96

Disbursements.

Expended for labor	$104 28
Expended for architect's service	1,958 65
Expended on contract with J. G. Naylor	29,868 44
Expended on contract with M. A. McGowan & Co	5,680 00
Expended for excavation and grading	587 72
Expended for mantels	505 00
Expended for iron-work	21 87
Expended for plumbing	1,345 00
Total	40,070 96

Estimates for next year.

The following estimates of appropriations for the service of the fiscal year ending June 30, 1878, have already been submitted.

1. For the support of the institution, including salaries and incidental expenses, and $500 for books and illustrative apparatus, $51,000.

2. For the completion of the work on the erection, furnishing, and fitting up of the buildings of the institution in accordance with plans heretofore submitted to Congress, $69,524.62.

3. For the inclosure, improvement, and care of the grounds of the institution, $10,000.

The estimate for the support of the institution will be found to be larger by three thousand dollars than the amount allowed annually for the last five years.

The completion of our buildings, which we hope will not be deferred longer than September of next year, will enable us to receive a larger number of students than we can now accommodate; and we have every indication that the applications for admission will be sufficiently numerous to justify the small increase of appropriation asked for. Should this prove to be an over-estimate, the whole amount need not be drawn.

We prefer, however, to avoid, if possible, any occasion for submitting an estimate hereafter to cover deficiencies.

With the building appropriation for the current year we shall be able to carry up the walls of the college-buildings to the window-lintels of the third story on the north division, and to roof in the south division, before the 1st of December. The estimates for the completion of the buildings have been made up with great care, and will, it is believed, be sufficient to cover the expense of connecting the new building with the completed sections, as well as the changes which will be necessary to make the roof of the old building correspond in style with that of the new.

If the appropriation we ask is made, our buildings will be finished at a cost very much within the general estimate submitted to Congress with our plans ten years ago.

The large increase in the number of our students, alluded to earlier in this report, renders it of the greatest importance that the college-buildings should be ready for occupancy by the last of September next.

The estimate submitted to provide for the proper inclosure and improvement of our grounds is of very great importance. No appropriation for this object has been made for several years, and our fences are in many places so decayed as to be at the mercy of every high wind.

The front line of our grounds on Boundary street has been so interfered with by the grading and curbing of the street as to present a very discreditable appearance, for the remedy of which we have no funds at our command.

THE APPROACHES TO THE INSTITUTION.

The rapid growth of the city towards the institution within the past few years, quickly following the grading of the streets in our vicinity, forces us to consider the subject of the approaches to our premises and the probable character of the permanent improvements on the squares separated from our grounds only by Boundary street.

These squares belong wholly to private owners, and may be built up at any time with improvements of a character quite unsuited to the near proximity of a public institution such as ours.

The instances are not few in our city, not to speak of other places from which many pointed illustrations might be drawn, where a very large expense has become necessary to secure appropriate surroundings to public buildings, the greater part of which expense might have been avoided by earlier action in the premises.

The squares lying along our front are not, it is true, needed for the actual uses of the institution; at the same time the interests of the institution and of the Government, as the holder of its property, would be very unfavorably affected should these squares be covered with permanent buildings of an inferior or objectionable character.

We feel, therefore, that we are only fulfilling the requirements of the law which makes it our duty to report on all matters affecting the interests of the institution committed to our care, when we urge the importance of action on the part of the Government, to secure the squares we have alluded to from improvements of an undesirable character.

They now have but very few buildings upon them, and the expense of purchasing all the space bounded by Sixth street east, L street, and Boundary, would be comparatively small.

And if we may be permitted to go so far as to suggest an important public interest outside the limits of our jurisdiction, that would be served by the securing to the Government of the ground just referred to, we may call attention to the fact that the large section of the city lying north of D street north and east of Fourth street west, comprising nearly two square miles, includes no public reservation whatever. The time is certainly not distant when it will contain a population large enough to claim the advantage of some public pleasure-ground; and for the purchase of land to form such a public square, no time is likely to be more favorable than the present, or immediate future.

SUPPORT OF STUDENTS FROM THE SEVERAL STATES.

In the history of our collegiate department a point has been reached when it seems proper to invite the governments of the several States to make provision for the support of students here. Hitherto our college work has been, in a measure, experimental, but the feasibility and importance of imparting a collegiate education to certain of the deaf of the country may now be considered as demonstrated. The testimony given on our last presentation-day by Professor Henry, of the Smithsonian Institution, and President Gilman, of the Johns Hopkins University, leaves no doubt as to the capability of deaf-mutes to complete what is understood by educators of the highest standing as the college curriculum. The positions taken in the world by our graduates as teachers, editors, public officials, &c., show plainly the value of the training they have received. We feel, therefore, justified in advising the governments of the several States to provide for the further education here of such pupils in their own institutions as may give evidence of ability to pursue a collegiate course, and prove themselves worthy to receive the assistance of their State in endeavoring to secure it.

To attempt to furnish in any State advantages equal to those offered here for the collegiate education of the deaf would involve an outlay many fold greater than would be incurred by sending the deaf-mutes of such States who might be proper subjects for advanced training to the National College. We feel, therefore, that in inviting the States to send beneficiaries here we are suggesting a measure of wise economy at the same time that we are offering them benefits not to be secured elsewhere. With the completion of our new building, next year, we shall have it in our power to accommodate twice as many students as are now in the college. We shall not, however, be able to provide for the support of the large proportion whose circumstances will be likely to compel them to ask for free admission.

It would seem, therefore, highly desirable that provision should be made for the support of such students by their own States.

In view of all these considerations, we venture to suggest that this subject be brought to the attention of the governors of the several States in some formal manner, so that the necessary steps may be soon taken to secure the requisite legislation.

All of which is respectfully submitted by order of the board of directors.

EDWARD M. GALLAUDET,
President.

HON. Z. CHANDLER,
Secretary of the Interior.

APPENDIX.

CATALOGUE OF STUDENTS AND PUPILS.

IN THE COLLEGE.

From Connecticut.—Herman Erbe, Warren Lacy Waters.
From Delaware.—Theodore Keisel.
From Illinois.—James Scott Fleming, Lester Goodman, Frank Ross Gray, Alva Jeffords, James Moline Tipton.
From Indiana.—James Irvin Sansom, Henry Edward Bierhaus.
From Iowa.—Frank Caleb Holloway, William Austin Nelson, George Moredock Teegarden.
From Kansas.—Frank Ashley Scott.
From Kentucky.—Dudley Webster George.
From Maine.—John Emery Crane, Edson Lancaster Kinney.
From Maryland.—Charles Stewart.
From Massachusetts.—Edwin Wellington Frisbie, Chester Quincy Mann, Albert Coleman Hargrave, John Albert Prince, Wilbur Norris Sparrow, Albert Samuel Tufts, Henry White, jr.
From Michigan.—Delos Albert Simpson, Edward Louis Van Damme.
From Minnesota.—James Martin Cosgrove, Jeremiah P. Kelley.
From Mississippi.—Robert Dameron Hazelett.
From New York.—William George Jones, William Albert Jackson, John Gordon Saxton.
From Ohio.—Samuel Mills Freeman, Robert King, Richard L' H. Long, Charles Merrick Rice, Albert Henry Schory, Frank Wiley Shaw, Lester Delos Waite, Alfred Flinn Wood.
From Pennsylvania.—Jerome Thaddeus Elwell, William Ellis Grime, Robert Middleton Zeigler.
From Tennessee.—Frank Alexander Branner, Isaac Newton Hammer, Minus C. E. Jordan, Thomas H. Wain.
From Vermont.—Frank Wilson Bigelow.
From Virginia.—John Walter Michaels.
From Wisconsin.—Lars M. Larson, James Joseph Murphy.
From District of Columbia.—Arthur Dunham Bryant.

IN THE PRIMARY DEPARTMENT.

FEMALES.

Mary M. Barnes	District of Columbia.
Carrie T. C. Cummings	Pennsylvania.
Louisa Yocum Fisher	District of Columbia.
Annie H. Elliott	South Carolina.
Katie Elliott	South Carolina.
Sarah A. Gourley	Maryland.
Mary Hawkins	District of Columbia.
Lydia Leitner	Maryland.
Caroline Mades	District of Columbia.
Elizabeth McCormick	Maryland.
Mary E. McDonald	District of Columbia.
Mary Pennybacker	District of Columbia.
Margaret Ryan	District of Columbia.
Josephine Sardo	District of Columbia.
Sophia R. Weller	District of Columbia.

MALES.

Wilber Fish Bateman	District of Columbia.
Edward T. Burns	District of Columbia.
Elmer E. Butterbaugh	District of Columbia.
Enoch G. Carroll	District of Columbia.
Edward Carter	District of Columbia.
Edmund Clark	District of Columbia.
Fred. C. Cook	Louisiana.
Wm. A. Connolly	District of Columbia.
Douglas Craig	District of Columbia.
Robert W. Dailey	District of Columbia.
John W. Dechard	District of Columbia.
Wm. F. Deeble	District of Columbia.
Abram Frantz	Pennsylvania.
Edgar Graugnard	Louisiana.
Thomas Haggerty	District of Columbia.
Edward Humphrey	District of Columbia.
Timothy Hyde	Delaware.
Jeremiah Hyde	Delaware.
Wm. Kohl	District of Columbia.
Frank Abraham Leitner	Maryland.
Joseph Lyles	District of Columbia.
John O'Rourke, jr	District of Columbia.
Columbus A. Rhea	Virginia.
Wm. J. Rich	District of Columbia.
Moses Robinson	District of Columbia.
Frank Ashley Scott	Kansas.
Calvin F. Stephens	Pennsylvania.
Henry Treischmann, jr	Maryland.
John W. L. Unsworth	District of Columbia.
Nelson White	District of Columbia.
Louis Whittington	District of Columbia.
Francis G. Würdemann	Kansas.

REGULATIONS.

I. The academic year is divided into three terms, the first beginning on the last Thursday in September, and closing on the 24th of December; the second beginning the 2d of January, and closing the last Thursday before Easter; the third beginning the first Tuesday after Easter, and closing the last Wednesday in June.

II. The vacations are from the 24th of December to the 2d of January, and from the last Wednesday in June to the last Thursday in September.

III. There are holidays at Thanksgiving and Easter.

IV. The pupils may visit their homes during the regular vacations, and at the above-named holidays, but at no other time, unless for some special, urgent reason, and then only by permission of the president.

V. The bills for the maintenance and tuition of pupils supported by their friends must be paid semi-annually, in advance.

VI. The charge for pay-pupils is $150 each per annum. This sum covers all expenses in the primary department except clothing, and all in the college except clothing and books.

VII. The Government of the United States defrays the expenses of those who reside in the District of Columbia, or whose parents are in the Army or Navy, provided they are unable to pay for their education. To students from the States and Territories who have not the means of defraying all the expenses of the college course, the board of directors renders such assistance as circumstances seem to require, as far as the means at its disposal for this object will allow.

VIII. It is expected that the friends of the pupils will provide them with clothing, and it is important that upon entering or returning to the institution they should be supplied with a sufficient amount for an entire year. All clothing should be plainly marked with the owner's name.

IX. All letters concerning pupils or application for admission should be addressed to the president.

○

www.ingramcontent.com/pod-product-compliance
Lightning Source LLC
Chambersburg PA
CBHW021622290326
41931CB00047B/1422
* 9 7 8 3 3 3 7 8 1 7 2 6 8 *